Monkey on the roof

Story by Margaret Clough
Illustrations by Naomi C. Lewis

"Look," said Matthew.

"Look at Monkey!"

"Up he goes," said Emma.

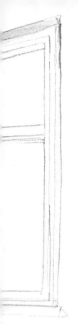

"Oh!" said Emma.

"Look at Monkey!

He is up on the roof."

"Monkey is up on the roof!"

shouted Emma.

"Come and look, Mom."

8

"I can see Monkey,"

said Matthew.

"Can I go up on the roof?"

Mom said,

"No, Matthew.

You can not go

up on the roof."

Mom went up the ladder.

"Here he is!" said Mom.

"Come down to me, Monkey,"

said Emma.

"Here he comes,"

said Matthew.

"Monkey went up on the roof,"

said Emma. "**Naughty Monkey!**"